Intimate Insights to Revolutionizing Intimacy

by Tziporah Kingsbury

A Pocketful book by Matrika Press

Copyright © Tziporah Kingsbury
December 2016

All Rights Reserved
including the right of reproduction of this book,
copying, or storage in any form or means, including
electronic, without prior written permission of the author.

ISBN 978-1-946088-85-7
Library of Congress Control Number:

1. Intimacy 2. Relationships 3. Sexuality 4. Breathwork
5. Spirituality 6. Title

Matrika Press
164 Lancey Street
Pittsfield, Maine 04967
(760) 889-5428

Editor@MatrikaPress.com

Matrika Press

First Edition

Printed in the USA

Coverart by Lucinda Rae

Arranged by "Twinkle" Marie Manning

Dear Reader,

Welcome to this opportunity to inspire new ways of conscious action and relating in the world. These insights are taken from my latest book "Revolutionizing Intimacy" - A Guide to Creating Profound Relationships From the Bedroom to The Boardroom to be released in 2017.

The intention through this intimate pocket book is to offer inspiration to revolutionize intimacy and shift the consciousness around the way we relate in our homes and the world.

The word "intimacy" seems to be shaded. With our attached stories and thousands of overwhelming perspectives, intimacy itself has been condemned to a small fragile box, with a very limited scope of reality for many people.

This is an invitation to deconstruct that box, remove the confining walls, and to expand on the infinite nature that rich authentic intimacy offers us.

This boundless form of intimacy is like an infinite garden without walls or borders. It is priceless material and wisdom to cultivate, cherish, and nourish.

Together, let's nurture a new garden within oneself. A garden that has healthy, vibrant soil, free to root down, feeling safe, and always grounded. A garden that will enable you to live your values, honor boundaries, be seen, be heard, and celebrated in all of life!

Revolutionizing Intimacy is essential in this world, where we have become so busy and overstimulated by loud and overwhelming environments. The world where people have forgotten how to feel, how to be. This world where many of us hide behind invented images and act how others view as "appropriate". Sadly, we have forgotten how to allow others deep inside our vulnerable places, inside our real self. Yet, how is someone able to allow another into such places, when they themselves are unable to find them, or don't even know they exist?

In our past, these places may have been judged as "inappropriate" for others to see, know about, or even discuss. This has created a vast separation amongst us. Deep down inside our souls, most of us yearn to be seen, to really feel, to be understood.

Humans desire to love, to feel, and to experience a deep spiritual connection with one another.

To Revolutionize Intimacy is the way to peace. Peace within oneself, peace within a community, within society, and the world. Many have been scarred by their imagined stories or conditioned beliefs of what intimacy is.

The depth of intimacy I am speaking of is a place where all the walls are torn down and there is no longer any hiding from yourself or others. There is no longer an inauthentic pretending to be someone you are not, in order to please another or yourself.

This sense of authenticity gifts one another permission to be you exactly as you/they are.

This quality of intimacy holds a realization of the interconnectedness of our inner world, the world around us, our body, our chi, and all other beings in the world.

With Love,
Tziporah

The Revolution of Intimacy is something to cultivate, to celebrate! When there is more collaboration, more communion, more celebration of each person's unique gifts, we will move from war to peace in everything we do.

Every moment we are relating to something or someone.
What degree of intimacy do you choose to experience?

The phenomenon of relationship is far too infinite to be contained within the walls of what society calls romance.

Relationship is a rite of passage that we are experiencing every moment with something or someone.

Every moment is an opportunity to create connection or separation. Which are you choosing?

The human species has only scratched the surface of the profound relationship with existence that we are capable of experiencing.
The time to emerge is now!

The degree to which you are aware and embodied defines the degree to which you experience intimacy.

The breath creates movement,
without it we are simply forcing
something by mere will.
One is life enhancing,
the other devours life.

Don't stop at being present with the food or the lover, yet go through it into a depth so far beyond thoughts and mind. They are a doorway to listen deeper, and to experience the expanding fields of life-force shared.

We have so many personas,
so many parts of our being that,
often, some parts get overshadowed,
lost and forgotten.
When this happens our life experiences
and relationships become dulled,
superficial and numbed.

Life is one of our greatest teachers. She is wise and she shows us lessons in every moment. The choice we have is whether or not we are present and alive enough to feel and listen to what she has to teach us.

If our gifts, our insights, our energy does not have an outlet, a resonating community or place to share, we will go into a toxic place of neediness.
A natural remedy is placing yourself in experiences that arouse and turn on your animal body and creativity.

It is not that those edgy moments or challenges aren't going to show up in life, the key is being able to have cultivated the present awareness and skills to navigate through it in a more conscious, mindful way.

No matter what your gender, race or sexual preference is, the inner masculine and feminine are shouting out and rising up to return to divine partnership with the warrior in each of us.

When we put our guard up so that we don't feel the anger, guilt, shame or sadness, etc., guess what happens? We end up in a tightly constructed suit of armor that walls in negative beliefs. We are left to stew with the belief that sex is bad and that our desires are wrong.

I am here to say that you matter! Your desires, your dreams, your feelings matter. You have a unique genius which the world needs. The way to finally feel the intimacy and the fullness of your sexuality is by going inward, into yourself and embracing the discomfort of old feelings and coming out on the other side; making sure every day to let your loved ones, friends, partner, community and the world know more about you, your desires, your dreams, and your feelings.

When was the last time you really
connected to your core values and
checked to see if the life you have
created was aligned with
what lights you up
in the depth of your being?
Is your animal body alive with
inspiration or is it experiencing
a slow death?

Be available for life.
Be available to look outside your pretty walls, or contained community to the bigger part of a community.
This is where life really begins.
This is where we can all make more of a difference simply by being available to love and to listen. The outcome is that we all feel more open and alive.

Sex is magic.
It is an unspoken language that
deserves reverence, understanding
and deep listening.
It is voice, it is expression and your
personal presence.
When you truly open yourself that way,
a force arises in you that has a presence
like a black-belt or a Samurai Warrior:
one graceful step takes you out of
harm's way, your decisions are decisive
and they align with your own body, mind,
sex and spirit.

To engage so deeply in sex, we must approach it from a holistic viewpoint. Sex is not a mere physical act where our genitals are touched to the point of orgasm. It is not even about reaching orgasm. You can go deeper!

When we open through sex we have the ability to feel the universe.
Sex is as mysterious as the universe, and at times that may feel scary,
intense, beautiful, and magically sweet all weaved together.

Relationship is one of the highest forms
of spiritual practice.

Your connection to your breath is
the most intimate relationship
you will ever have.

There is wisdom in your sexual evolution. Your sex has a voice and she wants to be acknowledged, heard and seen. Your sex is far bigger than you may imagine, so today, take another step, lean in, and embrace the power of your sexuality!

Your growth edge is where you explore all the most intricate pieces of your being, and have an opportunity to learn the most extraordinary things about yourself. Doing so means having more capacity to love and be loved.

Although relationships are not impervious to change, each connection is an exquisite gem that deserves devotion and honor. When relationships change it does not make the relationship (or the individuals involved) bad. Nor is it an excuse to run away or hide your love in fear.

Death and life are cyclical. You, my friend, change on a daily basis. It is essential to continue to cultivate your connection to yourself so that you are aware of these changes.

What would life and relationships look like if you let go of the disempowering agreements?

What if love and relationships never died, but rather, how they were expressed continuously changed like the season's, like nature.

You want to learn how to be a better lover, how to have better sex, how to communicate for success, how to trust more, how to have "real," "authentic" relationships.
Go deeper inside yourself and watch the magic unfold as you become naturally more intimately engaging with the world as a whole.

Your romantic and sexual fantasies only have the potential to be realized if you share them with your partner.

Your touch and gaze will endure when
it is done with presence and intention.
Flirtatiously brushing your body against
your lover's body while reaching for
the refrigerator door can set the tone
for the day. Run your hands over your
partner's bum or genitals as if it
were an accident as you head out
the door for work.

Any moment is a perfect moment for some surprise foreplay.
Foreplay outside of the bedroom is equally as important as it is inside, "play" being a key factor in relationship to yourself and your lover.
Make time for fun, silliness, joy, and laughter. You know… like you did in the beginning!

This boundless form of intimacy is like a infinite garden without walls or borders. It is priceless material and wisdom to cultivate, cherish, and nourish.

The more we live unguarded, learn to understand one another, feel our feelings, be aware of our "chi" flow, feel the flow of nature through and around us, the more our relationship with our body, our being, and others, moves from superficial to deeply rooted. We will move from a place of body wisdom to feeling wisdom. This is the place where true intelligence resides.

Curiosity and an authentic desire
to understand another opens the door
to deep connection and a sense of
intimate knowing.

Our breath is the most intimate relationship we will ever have the opportunity to experience.

Breath is the pathway of communication
with our physical and emotional body.
It is the communicator with our cells,
organs, and body chemistry.
It massages the organs via oxygen
carrying nutrients to the cells.
The way we breathe is affected by our
surroundings and affects the degree
one feels safe to intimately open
and create connection.

If we block this primary communication pathway of breath, it will have a vast effect on our actions, because it is so interrelated to the intelligence within our physical and emotional body.

Peace rather than war begins with communicating with yourself, by being present with your body and emotions. This mean returning to the most intimate relationship you have: the flow of your breath.

Understanding your conditioned breath pattern is a key to shifting the dysfunctional habits within your relationship with yourself and others.

Your breath gives you information so you may make a clear action-step to change. Re-training your breath will shift your quality of life, physically, mentally and emotionally. It will also effectively shift your relationships and the level of intimacy and connection you experience. Allow in a full breath now.

The awareness of your senses means
you are intimately getting to know the
most intricate places inside yourself.
To be able to make clear choices and
know your needs in the moment takes
awareness. It means moving through the
years of over-stimulation,
numbness, and a robotic nature
and into more presence.

When you begin to create more awareness, a sense of curiosity is birthed. The quality of curiosity leads to empowered change.

Deep physical intimacy with the self, becoming aware of what the body is sensing and perceiving is an open door into greater intimacy and connection with others.

When we are able to move out of the judgment stage of life — where we look at things from "right or wrong" — and into a deep desire to understand ourselves, others, and all of our feelings underneath the emotionally burdened stories, it opens up opportunity to create more effective communication.

When we feel invited to be involved,
we feel more compelled to listen.

Bottom line: we want our feelings to be
understood and our needs to be met!

The way to get what you want
is to get clear, direct and simple
in your communication.

I am here to say that emotions are one of your greatest allies. Your emotions are worthy of love and understanding, and you are going to share this new found love with them.

Your emotions are like messengers from your emotional body-intelligence letting you know it is needing something.
It wants to speak with you, to redirect you and let you know what this part of you is needing so it can move forward.
They are letting you know what might be off track in your relationship or your work projects.

Unattended emotions will create havoc in your relationships. They will hold onto you so tightly that you feel frozen and unable to access the level of fulfillment and connections you want in sharing your soul's purpose.

Vulnerability is sexy!

Communication has the power to create connection and intimacy, or disconnection, separation and even war. What are you going to choose?

The point when you make a relationship about what you are getting versus what you are sharing can be the end point of any relationship.

Your responsibility is to commit to living in a clear, uplifted state. Our partners, our colleagues, our friends are not responsible for doing what we want, or making us happy.

A glitch in relationships of any kind takes place when you enter into the relationship thinking it — or the person or people — are there to fill your void, your needs, your wants. It now becomes about you verse's the relationship as a whole.

Being selfish means making so much compromise that you are now being untrue to the core of who you are, your values and your needs.
This is not caring for the relationship body, it is actually creating a slow death of the relationship.

When we make a choice to be in a
relationship and for it to truly be
one that is empowering all people
involved, it means honoring
the seasons of change.
We change on a daily basis.
There are many degrees
to which this change happens
and what it affects.

The beauty of a relationship is that we get to learn and grow together. The magnificence of life is the union of the Divine and our natural human-ness. Living in these human bodies offers human needs and universal feelings. To deny this basic fundamental truth can wreak havoc emotionally and create more separation in our relationships.

Relationships are mirrors to show us our
many aspects of being — our emotions,
our shadow side and yes, even
our glorious light.

Relationship is like creating art.
It is a canvas fresh and clean for you to create how you desire. Explore your personal boundaries, edges, desires, concerns and fears. Support each other to continue to expand and evolve into new infinite fields of love.
Be patient and play a lot. Watch for getting stuck in a process.

If our sexual energy/creative life force is the fuel that births not just babies, but anything we desire to create in our world, would it not hold an immense amount of information, wisdom and experience to learn from?

Sexuality is magic, it is creative, it is life-force and it is calling us to listen.

When we feel arousal or sensations which feel good, we usually focus on building it, heading for the goal. However arousal naturally rises and falls like the waves in the ocean. It is in riding each wave that pleasure builds, prolongs and becomes a state of being rather than a quick blissed-out moment.

All relationships thrive when there is awareness, presence, play and fun. This is especially applicable in the bedroom!

A functional relationship is one where there is security starting from inside oneself, emotional stability, clear communication, absence of manipulation or harm to another, the ability to say "no" without fear of losing something or "yes" without the fear of being rejected.

What is so beautiful about creating more intimacy around the discussion of your sexual desires is creating freedom and liberation. You are able to own your sexuality. Here, there is no longer a need to hide behind a world of shame, guilt, embarrassment or fear of what you desire.

Relationships no longer become about "You complete me," or that "white picket fence," yet now holds a quality of "how can we together walk empowered in who we are;" "how may I evolve to live clearer, more centered, aware;" and "how can we allow this love of relating to influence the greater good in the world?"

Absence makes the heart, sex, body and soul grow fonder indeed!

Even in the most brilliant, juiciest, passionate partnerships, the creating of self-space and solo-time are essential nutrients in order to grow the garden of your relationship.

Intimacy contains various qualities that allows us to feel deeply, to awaken all the senses and acknowledge, in some way, an interconnection with the people and environment around us.
It allows you to feel as if you are permeating the existence of all things.
It is deep knowing, and being known.

Sensuality is the awakening of the senses. It is where a person indulges in feeling and allows his feelings to guide his actions.

We must feel into order to create
sustainable change.

To really understand what is important
to you, your body, mind, sex and spirit
you must fully inhabit the body.

Life is always inspiring in your favor.
The Key is to get out of the way,
breathe her in and let life rapture you.

Change is your ally, allow it to swiftly cut through the old debris and clutter that is no longer serving you or your relationships. Be still, present with deep trust and courage. This is part of your grand evolution to live more fully and love more boldly!

When you commit to having an intimate relationship with yourself, one that frees and empowers you in body, mind and spirit, you will have the capacity to connect deeply with others from a place of power and authenticity.

ABOUT THE AUTHOR

Tziporah Kingsbury, Founder of the Soulful Relating Institute, is a world-renowned transformational leader, inspirational speaker and innovator in the realm of intimacy and relationships.

Author of the upcoming book *Revolutionizing Intimacy*, she is most recently known for being featured on *ABC's The Bachelor* and called *"America's Love Guru."*

Creator of the Soulful Relating 7-Step System™, Tziporah specializes in guiding her clients in awakening spiritually, sensually and sexually, so they can create profound relationships from the bedroom to the boardroom.

Tziporah's vision is to embody and support others in cultivating an unprecedented level of presence and radical aliveness, be it in their private or professional life.

She is passionate about pioneering new edges around the way we relate in the world.. Tziporah believes this intensity of devotion and joy is what is needed at this time in the world, in our families, communities and on the political stage.

Learn about Tziporah's *"Soulful Relating 7-Step System"* at:
http://www.tziporahintimacy.com/thesoulfulrelating7stepsystem/

www.tziporahintimacy.com
www.soulfulrelatinginstitute.com

NEW BOOK COMING IN 2017

This book, *Revolutionizing Intimacy* is the "how" in reconnecting you on spiritual, emotional, and physical planes. It's wisdom shares the realization that all relationships stem from our own center. The greatest responsibility when entering in relationship either in the warmth of your own home or in the work environment is cultivating a rich relationship with oneself—body, mind and spirit. The benefits to creating this kind of relationship with yourself are priceless:

  - You exude presence, awareness, and sensitivity
  - You take ownership for all parts of yourself, your emotions, your triggers and reactions.
  - You embody and actually become the inter-relating skills we will speak of in this book and allow them to simply be the means of changing relationships and relating in the world.

www.tziporahintimacy.com/books

ABOUT THE COVER ARTIST

Lucinda Rae is an award-winning artist and spiritual creative entrepreneur. As a prosperity brand mentor and visibility coach, she has created over 200 brand identities over 17 years for both corporate and spiritual entrepreneurs, and has captured thousands of stunning images in her photography. She is the founder and artist of *Light Divine*, devoted to bringing a *Touch of Heaven* to your home.

She is a *Soul Art® Guide* for spiritual awakening, creative expression, healing, and expanded magic for increased life magnetism and meaning.

Lucinda believes every person's journey is to be fully expressed as the Light that we are and share that in the realms of beauty, purity and passion in this precious life.

www.Lucinda-Rae.com

ABOUT MATRIKA PRESS

Matrika Press is an independent publishing house dedicated to publishing works in alignment with Unitarian Universalist values and principles. Its fiscal sponsor is UU Women and Religion. (www.uuwr.org)

Matrika derives its name from the 50 letters of the Sanskrit alphabet called "the mothers" aka "Matrika." Kali Ma used the letters to form words, and from the words formed all things...as with the Bible: *"in the beginning was the Word."*

People of all backgrounds and faiths agree: *Words are powerful.*
More than that: *Their vibrations are creative forces; they bring all things into being.*

Matrika Press publishes anthologies, memoirs, poetry, prayer and ritual manuscripts, and other books to bring transformation to the world.

We *do* accept unsolicited manuscripts at this time. Should you wish to Publish your work, visit our website.

www.MatrikaPress.com

AVAILABLE NOW FROM MATRIKA PRESS

This book is a compilation of women sojourners, sages, mystics, witches, shaman, medicine women, ministers, philosophers, therapists, life coaches, yogis, and more. Their journeys. Their stories. Their teachings and practices. Essays, Poetry, Art, Rituals and Prayers. This anthology is full of useful tools and powerful messages for everyone who is on a spiritual journey to embrace and enjoy. Beloved Contributors include:
- *Anna Huckabee Tull • Bernadette Rombough • Deb Elbaum*
- *Deborah Diamond • Debra Wilson Guttas • Grace Ventura*
- *Janeen Barnett • JoAnne Bassett • Judy Ann Foster*
- *Julie Matheson • Kate Early • Kate Kavanagh • Katherine Glass*
- *Kris Oster • Lea M. Hill • Meghan Gilroy • Morwen Two Feathers*
- *Rustie MacDonald • Shamanaca • Sharon Hinckley • Shawna Allard*
- *Shiloh Sophia • Susan Feathers • Tiffany Cano • Tory Londergan*
- *"Twinkle" Marie Manning • Tziporah Kingsbury • Valerie Sorrentino*

www.MatrikaPress.com

Seventh Principle Studies & First Source Explorations

The Seventh
Unitarian Universalist Principle is:
*"Respect for the interdependent web
of all existence of which we are a part."*

The First Source Unitarian Universalists draw
faith from is: *"Direct experience of that transcending mystery
and wonder, affirmed in all cultures, which moves us to a
renewal of the spirit and an openness to the forces
which create and uphold life."*

Evidence to support such is found within the
pages of ***The Way of Power***.

www.MatrikaPress.com

ALSO FROM MATRIKA PRESS

www.MatrikaPress.com

RECOMMENDED SELECTIONS FROM SKINNER HOUSE

Reaching for the Sun
Rev. Angela Herrera's book of meditations, prayers and invocations provide inspiration to readers and serve as a resource to those seeking powerful liturgical words, grounded in the experiences of everyday life.

Evening Tide
This book of mediations by Elizabeth Tarbox helps readers to face the darker moments of life, the challenging circumstances that call us to live more fully even when we feel our most empty.

Stirring the Nation's Heart: Eighteen Stories of Prophetic Unitarians and Universalists of the 19th Century by Polly Peterson
Eighteen compelling stories from the lives of some of the nineteenth-century Transcendentalists and reformers who played key roles in Unitarian Universalist history.

http://www.uua.org/publications/skinnerhouse

RECOMMENDED SELECTIONS FROM BEACON PRESS

Claiming the Spirit Within
This wonderful book, edited by Rev. Marilyn Sewell, is a beautiful sourcebook of poetry and prose. A rich and diverse anthology dedicated to the praise of life, it presents the sacredness that emerges when women immerse fully in living lives of spirit while embracing the physical. More than 300 poems celebrating all aspects of women's lives.

http://www.beacon.org/

ISBN 978-1-946088-85-7

www.ingramcontent.com/pod-product-compliance
Lightning Source LLC
Chambersburg PA
CBHW071537080526
44588CB00011B/1708